MARRYING A

WIDWER

MARRYING A
WIDWER

WHAT YOU NEED TO KNOW
BEFORE TYING THE KNOT

ABEL KEOGH

BEN LOMOND
PRESS

Published by
Ben Lomond Press
Copyright © 2012 by Abel Keogh
All rights reserved

Cover design by Francine Eden Platt of Eden Graphics, Inc.
Cover design Copyright © 2012 by Abel Keogh

Opinions expressed in this book are those of the author.
ISBN 10: 0615632602
ISBN 13: 978-0615632605

TABLE OF CONTENTS

INTRODUCTION

IF YOU'VE JUST STARTED dating a widower, this book may not be for you—it's for women who are in a serious relationship with a widower and are thinking about spending the rest of their lives with him. To know whether or not the man you're interested in is prepared to enter the dating world, I suggest you first read *Dating a Widower: Starting a Relationship with a Man Who's Starting Over*. That book gives you a frame of reference so you can determine if he is mentally and emotionally ready to move on. *Marrying a Widower* will help you know whether he's prepared to make the ultimate commitment and spend the rest of his life with you. More importantly, it will walk you through many of the unique circumstances and challenges that come with marrying a widower to help you decide if taking this step is right for *you*.

Throughout this book, I'm going to assume that marriage is the eventual end game of your dating activities. I understand that not everyone wants to get married. Some people are happy with lifelong partnerships or something else—that's fine too. If you don't want to tie the knot, as you read this book, just replace the word "marriage" with a term that describes what you want the relationship to become.

Having a successful marriage takes a lot of work. As long as you're both willing to make each other the center of your universe and invest the time, energy, and love it takes to grow and nurture your relationship, you will have a partnership that will bring you nothing but joy and that will last for the rest of your life.

I hope this book can help you decide if marrying a widower is the right thing to do, or that it can help make your current marriage (if you've already married a widower) sweeter and stronger.

Abel Keogh
April 2012

CHAPTER 1

THE END GAME

WIDOWERS BECOME INVOLVED in serious relationships for different reasons. Some miss the late wife and want someone to "be there" to help alleviate the empty feeling in their lives. Others want someone who will be on call for an occasional roll in the hay, to cook their meals, or to babysit their kids. And, believe it or not, there are even widowers who are looking for someone they can spend the rest of their lives with. Whatever his reason for wanting a relationship, it's important that you both have the same end game in mind. For example, if you want to get married, but he prefers living together, or he'd be happy with a nebulous, open-ended friendship, you're going to waste months or years of your life with someone who's never going to give you the love and happiness you deserve.

While it's important to be on the same page in any relationship, it's doubly important to make sure a widower has the same relationship goals. Many men will settle for a relationship with a woman they don't love simply because they're lonely. Almost every widower I've talked to has, at some point, started a serious relationship because they wanted companionship. These widowers keep the relationship going until they tire of it or until someone better comes along. They leave behind lots of broken hearts and women who feel used.

Sadly, I've made this very mistake. Less than a year after my wife, Krista, took her own life, I became serious with a good friend named Jennifer. I promised her the world and implied a life of happiness together. I started that relationship because my heart ached for companionship, and having someone in my life who wasn't a perfect fit was still a hundred times better than being alone.

When things started to get serious with Jennifer, I thought I loved her—or at least, I had strong feelings that I thought would turn into love. It was nice to have someone to talk to and a warm body to hold, even if I couldn't see myself spending the rest of my life with her. As time went on and my feelings for her only become more ambivalent, I tried to convince myself that I loved her. I rationalized my lack of love toward her as a sign that I was still grieving. All I needed, I thought, was more time to grieve, and things would eventually work out. It wasn't until Julianna came along that I realized I never really loved Jennifer in the first place.

If you want to avoid being the woman who gets used by a lonely widower, you need to make absolutely sure you and he both want to get married—to each other. The sooner you can do that, the better off you'll both be.

There are several ways to know how the widower really feels about you. The best and most obvious way is through his actions—not his words. If he always treats you like a queen, it's a good sign that he wants to spend the rest of his life with you. But more often than not, a widower will send mixed signals. For example, he may call you every day, but still have photographs of the late wife all over the house. Or he may wine and dine you every night, but won't stop talking about the late wife and the fantastic life they shared together. This makes it hard for a woman to know where she stands.

Find time when the two of you can have a serious conversation about where you see the relationship going. This can be a scary step, because there's always a chance the widower may not give you the answer you want. But knowing the truth, even if you don't like it, is better than wasting part of your life with someone who is with you because he doesn't want to be alone.

Keep in mind that one talk probably won't do it, either. Julianna and I had several big talks at different points in our relationship. We had our first conversation about six weeks after becoming exclusive, another when Julianna realized I was still wearing a necklace with Krista's ring on it, a third when I accidently called Julianna by Krista's name, and a fourth during a six-hour drive home from a marathon she ran. There were probably lots of smaller talks in between, too. Sometimes I found them uncomfortable, because Julianna was worried about whether I was really ready to commit. However, because we were able to openly discuss what we wanted from the relationship, our discussions helped us move toward our goal of marriage.

Knowing that she wanted to spend the rest of her life with me made it easier for me to make room in my heart for her. It also helped me focus on starting a new life with her and served as a gut check to ensure it was something I really wanted to do. The more we talked about marriage, the more excited we became about taking a walk down the aisle together. So when I finally did ask Julianna to marry me, the proposal itself wasn't a total surprise. We'd talked enough that she knew I'd eventually ask her to marry me, and that when I did, she would say "Yes!"

How Soon Should You Have the Talk?

Over the years, I've had people ask me how long they should wait before having this talk with the widower. The truth is, there's no set timeframe. As a rule of thumb, if you've been seriously dating for several months and you can see yourself marrying him, there's nothing wrong with bringing up the subject—and it doesn't matter how long the late wife has been dead, either. Julianna and I had our first "Where is this relationship going?" talk about a month after we started dating seriously, about nine months after I became a widower.

Don't worry about having the talk too soon and scaring him away. You're both adults, and you should be able to have adult conversations. Talking about the future isn't a proposal. It doesn't mean you have to get married the next day. It's better to know sooner, rather than later, if you both want to get married, so you can work toward that goal or move on with your lives.

Know What You Want Before You Talk

Before you talk about your future together, it's vital that you know where you see the relationship going. Do you want to get married, or do you want something more casual? If you can't clearly define what you want from the relationship, don't bring up the subject until you can. It's unfair to the widower to expect him to talk about a possible future together if you don't know what you want.

Beware of the Grief Card

Widowers willing to settle for companionship with women they don't love will often play the grief card when talks about the future arise. They'll say things like they're still grieving, or that they need more time before they can figure out what they want. If a single or divorced man said something similar, most women would hesitate to take the relationship any further. Widowers, however, tend to be given more leniency when it comes to opening their hearts, and a woman will move forward despite the widower's inability to articulate how he really feels about her and the relationship.

The truth is, widowers know how they feel about the woman they're with. Those who know they want to get married again don't have a hard time saying it—even if they're still mourning the late wife. I dated Julianna less than a year after Krista's death. My heart was still tender, and I was still grieving. There were times before or after a date with Julianna when I'd cry my eyes out. Despite being an emotional wreck at times, I knew I didn't want to spend my life with anyone but Julianna. I also knew that the only thing keeping us from getting married was my own sorrow and sadness, so I worked as hard as I could to forgive Krista and move on with my life. I did it because I knew that the reward of taking

Julianna by the hand and exchanging vows would be well worth it. Widowers who feel the same way about you will do the same. A widower unable to make room in his heart for the woman he's dating has no business being involved in a serious relationship.

WIDOWERS ACT HOW THEY REALLY FEEL

Sometimes it's hard to distinguish between widowers looking for companionship and those who want to get married. The best way to know how he really feels about you is to pay attention to his actions, not his words. Any widower can proclaim his love, or say he wants to spend the rest of his life with you. Only a widower who really loves you will treat you like the only woman he's ever loved. Widowers who talk a good talk, but don't really have your best interests in mind, will eventually betray themselves through their own actions.

When I was dating Jennifer, I said lots of wonderful things I didn't mean. For a while, I was able to back up my sweet nothings with actions: I called her every night, flew down to see her on a regular basis (we lived several hundred miles apart), and sent her emails throughout the day. But eventually, I couldn't put the physical effort into the story I'd weaved. I stopped calling her as often, made excuses why I couldn't fly down, and sent fewer and fewer emails. Despite this, I continued to tell her that we had a future together, and she continued to believe it.

If you have any doubt about how the widower really feels about you, pay close attention to how he treats you. Those who are sincere about tying the knot will align their actions with their words. They'll do everything in their power to make you feel like the only woman they've ever loved. Widowers who are in relationships for their own selfish reasons will be able to put on an act for only so long. With these men, sooner or later, you feel like you're competing with a ghost.

Have the Courage to Walk Away

If you believe he doesn't have the same relationship goals as you do, don't be afraid to walk away. Some women hold on to a relationship that's not going anywhere because they think the widower will change his mind or eventually grow to love them. Don't fall into this trap. Love doesn't work that way. If he can't fall in love with you after several months or so of serious dating, he never will.

Never settle for a relationship with anyone who can't give you top billing in his heart and mind. If you settle for second place, you'll never be truly happy. Life is too short to waste on someone who can't treat you like you deserve to be treated. If you wait for the widower to come to his senses, the relationship will eventually end, and you'll have nothing to show for it. Have the courage to walk away. You're a queen and deserve to be treated as such.

CAROL'S STORY

When I first met my husband, he was 45 and widowed less than a year. I was 43 and crazy about him, but also quite lonely.

He talked constantly about his deceased wife. At first, I tried to be sympathetic because I liked him so much. After a few weeks, (yes, I was still seeing him, despite the enormous red flag) I finally told him I was sick of hearing about her. I didn't care what she would have done in such-and-such situation, I didn't care what she liked and didn't like, and I sure as heck didn't care that she had ugly feet! I also didn't care if he stuck around or not.

But stick around he did, and being the lonely, bored woman I was, I continued to see him. Over time he talked about the late wife less and less. Occasionally she came up in conversation, but she seemed to be mostly on the way out. I hoped that our relationship would be finally one of two hearts instead of three. Unfortunately, my happiness would prove to be short lived.

After four years of dating, we decided to get married, despite all the red flags—for example, when I first met his mother, we traveled hundreds of miles and stayed in her house. The first day, I found myself alone with her. His mother's opening line? "So, you knew Mary [the late wife], didn't you?" Then I sat and listened to hours of what Mary did and liked. His mother never asked anything about me—where I worked, what my family was like, nothing. Not only that, but the bedroom in her house where I stayed had pictures of Mary and her husband all over the walls. It was horrible.

Now we have been married two years, and the deceased wife is back with a vengeance. I recently found out that when I am at work, my husband goes to the cemetery and takes pictures of himself next to their double plot. I was crushed and felt like number two all over again.

Ladies, do not make the mistake I did. I wanted to believe that things would get better with time. Do not be in denial if the man you are with is still hung up on a deceased spouse. All people deserve to be number one in their spouse's life. Do not settle. If you see these types of red flags, *run away as fast as you can*. At nearly 50 years old, I'll have to go through another divorce and start over again, all because I wanted to kid myself that things would get better. My husband's first wife has been dead seven years, and things have only gotten worse. Take off the rose-colored glasses and find someone who cherishes you for who you are. You'll be glad you did.

CHAPTER 2

TALK, TALK, TALK:
THE IMPORTANCE OF COMMUNICATION

BEFORE YOU MARRY a widower, you need to be comfortable talking about anything and everything, including the late wife, his grief, and any other widower-related issues. There's a tendency to think that subjects about his past and moving on are off limits, or can only be addressed if he brings them up.

Not true.

If you're going to get married, both of you need to be comfortable talking about these subjects. While you should always be considerate when talking about the late wife or other sensitive issues, there's nothing that says you can't or shouldn't talk about them. If you can't address them, you'll struggle to know if he really loves you and is ready to start a new life.

Women often worry about an issue only to find out it can easily be solved by just talking about it. Let me give you one example: A woman who had been dating a widower for several months emailed me with a problem. The birthday of the widower's late wife was coming up in two days. As the late wife was dying, the widower promised her that he and their three children would honor her memory every year on her birthday by baking a cake. To make an uncomfortable situation even more difficult, the widower was going to be out of town on his late wife's birthday, and the woman was going to be left alone with his children. She asked me if she should continue the tradition or let the widower take care of it after he returned.

I asked if she'd talked about it with him. She said she hadn't, because she didn't know how to bring it up. We talked about some different ways to approach the situation, and she told me she'd get back to me and let me know how things went. The next day, she reported on their conversation. She'd told him that she had a hard time with the tradition and couldn't do it by herself—however, she would be happy to support him in upholding this tradition if it was something he wanted to continue. Much to her surprise, the widower said that they didn't have to do anything to commemorate that day, because he was in a relationship with her and was moving on. The woman, to say the least, was very relieved.

If you haven't figured out how to communicate with your widower, both of you need to work on learning how to start and conduct meaningful conversations. Talking things out can often solve issues before they become a problem. And it's not just widower issues you need to address, but any other issue that affects you as couple. There shouldn't be anything in your relationship you can't tackle.

I had to work on learning how to communicate with Julianna. She came from a family that was very open and communicative on almost any topic. My family was more reserved—we never talked about certain things. I learned the hard way just how open Julianna's family is when I first met them. We were sitting in their family room talking, and one of her sisters brought up the fact I was a widower and asked how I was dealing with it—in front of the entire family. I looked around and saw seven pairs of eyes staring back at me, waiting for my answer. An open conversation about someone's marital status never would have happened in my family.

On the drive home, I told Julianna how surprised I was that her family knew so much about me. I told her that the situation had somewhat embarrassed me, because I didn't know how to handle it. Julianna explained how communication worked in her family and that openness and honesty was what she needed from me in order to marry me. When I told her I wasn't used to being so open, she simply shrugged and said I needed to learn how to do it, or our relationship wouldn't go much further.

Julianna was diplomatic and loving. Her words didn't sound like an ultimatum (even though they were), and she also let me know she was willing to be patient and work with me. But at the same time, she was very clear that she wouldn't waste time with me if I kept secrets or held things back.

It took a lot of work to learn how to talk about anything and everything with Julianna, but I'm glad we did. Having open and honest communication strengthened our relationship and helped us move toward marriage, because we both had a better idea of how I was coping, how Julianna was dealing with my past, and other widower issues.

Knowing how to talk to each other has done more than anything else to keep our marriage strong. If something's bothering one of us, we can talk about it. Even though widower-related issues don't come up nearly as often as they did a decade ago, we don't have a problem discussing them when a question arises. We can talk about money, sex, children, family, religion, politics, or anything else that comes up. Even if we don't always agree on a solution, we both know that we're there for each other and will work through anything.

Widowers Aren't Fragile

There's a common misconception that you need to treat a widower with kid gloves when it comes to talking about grief, moving on, or other issues. This is a false idea and can be destructive. If a widower has agreed to a serious relationship, he's also agreed to enter the dating world, where he'll be treated like anyone else. Don't let his marital status intimidate you from having conversations about the relationship. Remember— he's the one who decided to get into a relationship.

That's not to say you should be disrespectful of his past, but you shouldn't think you can't talk to him about moving on and starting a new life just because his wife died. Widowers who are serious about you and a future with you won't have a problem talking about these things. For me, the conversation was one I wanted to have with Julianna soon after we become serious so I could let her know how I felt, but also so I could gauge her feelings about things.

The fact that someone has lost a spouse doesn't give them the right to be treated differently than others. Some widowers are simply content to have a live-in maid, babysitter, and mistress all rolled into one. If you don't mind that kind of relationship, that's fine. But if you're looking for marriage or a lifelong partnership, don't settle for someone who doesn't want the same thing. If you settle, you're in for nothing but a life of heartache and disappointment.

A Word of Caution:
Widowers Aren't Your Girlfriend

One thing you need to remember is that widowers are men. That means they communicate like men—not like your girlfriend. When you are encouraging him to open up to you about things, don't expect him to talk to you like your girlfriend does.

For example, I received an email from a woman who had been married to a widower for several years. When the anniversaries of the late wife's death and her birthday rolled around, the widower withdrew for a day or two, and then life would return to normal. The woman, however, became stressed about it every time. She kept pressuring him to open up about his feelings and "do something" about it when those days happened, thinking it might help him if he had some way to get his sad feelings out of his system. Finally, the widower gave in to her demands and went to the cemetery, accompanied by his new wife. On the way back, all he could do was talk about his past life and things he and the late wife had done together. By the time the couple arrived home, the woman was nearly in tears, because she felt like her husband no longer loved her.

I completely understood why the woman felt the way she did, but I couldn't help wondering if she hadn't brought some of this on herself. Because the widower didn't open up to her in the way that her best friend or other girlfriends did, she thought something was wrong. The result was an outpouring of memories and feelings that emotionally devastated her and nearly ended their marriage.

Be ye not so stupid.

While it's true that Julianna and I have an open and honest relationship and can talk to each other about anything, we've both learned when and how to approach the other person, and how to communicate. Julianna knows that if I've had a tough day at work or I'm feeling stressed about something, she can ask once what's bothering me. If I don't want to talk about it just then, she'll give me time to cool down and work things out. She knows that when I've had time to mull things over in my mind, I'll come back, and we'll pick up the conversation where we left off. She understands that I don't talk like her mom, her sisters, or her best friend. Similarly, I know that if she's had a rough day with the kids, I need to give her time to exercise or read so she can get to a point where she's willing to discuss what's on her mind.

Every person has his or her personal quirks and way of communicating. The challenge the two of you face is finding a way to talk about things that works for both of you. What works for one couple may not for another. It may be challenging and hard at times to figure it out, but I promise that if you can work out the communication aspect of your relationship, it will save you heartache and trouble for as long as the two of you are together. Aside from watching his actions, talking to your widower is the next best way of knowing if he's really ready to move on and start a new life with you.

JESSICA'S STORY

Ryan and I both lost our spouses to brain cancer within four days of each other. While I was laying my 33-year-old husband to rest, he was watching his 30-year-old wife take her last breath. We both blogged through our journeys, he from Oklahoma, and I from Michigan. We didn't know each other or follow each other's blogs.

Then a woman in Tennessee who followed both our blogs left a comment on my blog suggesting that I check out his, because we had similar stories and shared the commonality of having several young children. One thing led to another, which led to a pretty quick marriage nine months after our meeting and a very foolish idea that we would grieve beautifully together.

We did grieve together, although it wasn't always so beautiful. Early on, we thought we would share everything—all our feelings, our hurts, and our bad days. Soon we realized that this wasn't such a great idea. It was extremely difficult to hear about my husband's grief over another woman, and, although he was more sympathetic about it with me, he didn't handle hearing about my late husband very well either.

We decided that we would do our grieving in private and remember the good times together. We rationalized that in our past marriages, we never would have shared all of the intimate details of a previous relationship with our late spouses, so why would we put the intimate details of a previous marriage on our current spouses? We also made an active choice to be happy.

We realized that we could relive our painful pasts over and over again through pictures, reading the blogs, and watching videos, but we instead chose to remember the good and learn from the past. We are both grateful for such wonderful first marriages, but realize that we often took them for granted. We are adamant about not making that mistake again with each other.

We live every moment of our lives together in thankfulness for our health and for each other. Part of the process for us in securing a marriage between just the two of us was to remove most of our late spouses' belongings from our new home. For us, it needed to be *our* house. The kids all have special memorabilia in their rooms—pictures and keepsakes—but in terms of the house, our bedroom, and my kitchen, their stuff was (for the most part) packed up and put away in the attic for the kids to have someday.

A romantic but misleading idea says that love never dies. But love does pass on when the widow or widower is ready to start anew. Even though I miss my late husband, a man who was my best friend for ten years, and Ryan misses his late wife just as much, we had to put our love for our late spouses to rest. Society allows divorced people to say that their love died, but if someone literally dies, widows and widowers are not given the same permission to feel that way. However, Ryan and I both strongly feel that spousal love needs to be reciprocated. If someone is not ready to put that love to rest and "bury it," so to speak, then they're probably not ready to move on. It's never fair for anyone in a relationship to feel like he or she is competing with an imaginary ghost of a former spouse.

We will always love what we had with our late spouses, but in the past tense. We respect and honor the roles they played in our lives and in our children's lives, but the reality is that they are gone. Emotionally, physically, and spiritually, our marriage is about the two of us. Ours is not a happy marriage of four, as some would say—it is a happy marriage of two.

We both try very hard not to bring spousal comparisons into our relationship, but only remembrances of our best friends. In the first months of our marriage, I struggled with my own comparisons (and those implied by others) of how I raised the kids, my organizational skills (or lack thereof), my cooking, and on and on, but Ryan never put that on me. He let me talk my

feelings through, write through it, and he always listened, and then he told me I was full of it and reassured
me through words, actions, letters, and love that I was
the one and only.

I do believe that if we would have dated a little bit
longer, those issues would have been worked out in the
dating process, but due to our long-distance romance
and having a total of seven children involved, we chose
to get married fast, and we chose to work through our
issues under the banner of a marriage commitment. I
can honestly say that today, ten months married, most
of these issues and comparisons aren't there anymore.
Ryan has done a wonderful job of making me feel like
the love of his life in this moment and time.

CHAPTER 3

THE LATE WIFE'S FAMILY

WHEN YOU TIE THE KNOT, for better or worse, you marry into your spouse's family. If your spouse happens to be a widower, the late wife's family ends up being part of your life as well. How big of a role they play depends on the relationship the widower had with them before she died, the age of kids—if any—from the first marriage, how close the in-laws live to the widower, and how much the widower relied on them after his late wife passed on. Whether you see them once a year or several times a month, having the late wife's family in your life can make it difficult to feel like you're starting a new journey together.

It's impossible for me to dictate how involved the

late wife's family should be, because what's okay for one person may not be acceptable for someone else. For example, at the end of this chapter, you'll find a story from someone who practically lives next door to the late wife's family and has a great relationship with them. Others would have a difficult time living so close to her family and wouldn't get along with them as well.

What I *can* do is give you four things to think about as you make the determination for yourself.

YOU SHOULD ALWAYS FEEL LIKE NUMBER ONE

The widower chose to marry you, but that doesn't mean he's suddenly going to forget about the late wife's family and the role these people have played in his life. Unless he was on extremely bad terms with the late wife's family, it's impossible to expect them to stop being part of his life, or not to keep in touch to some extent—especially if there are minor children from their marriage still living at home. For better or worse, they're part of his extended family, which means you may be invited to holidays, family events, or Sunday dinners. But no matter how much time you or he spends with her family, you should always feel like the center of the widower's universe. You should never feel like he's letting them come between the two of you, or that the amount of time and activities they're a part of interferes with your marriage.

Widowers who accept invitations to spend time with the former in-laws, or take their kids to visit Grandma and Grandpa, don't love the late wife more, or wish they hadn't remarried. If you feel like activities with the late wife's family are coming between you and your potential husband, examine where those feelings are coming from. Are you simply experiencing internal insecurity, or do you really feel he'd rather be with them instead of you? If it's the latter, you need to talk to the widower about it and solve it *before* you tie the knot—not after. You both need to agree to set up some parameters. Whatever you decide, he should be the one to communicate it to the late wife's family to avoid hard feelings or misunderstandings that might arise if you were to tell them.

Though Julianna never felt like number two on the occasions we have spent time with members of Krista's family, there were times when she felt uncomfortable because she accurately sensed that many of them had a hard time seeing me moving on with another woman so quickly. Things got a little better the longer we were together, but it was an issue that truly never resolved, because we moved after getting married, and we didn't spend much time with Krista's family after that. To spend time with the late wife's family, it's important to understand your own insecurities and not let them come between the widower and the late wife's family. Spending time with them doesn't mean he's stopped loving you.

People Change; Relationships Evolve

Relationships aren't static. The decisions we make on a day-to-day basis affect our relationships for better or worse. When we marry someone, that person becomes the center of our universe, and the relationships we have with others become secondary. When a widower remarries, that means his relationship with the late wife's family has to change as well. Though he can still interact with them, it can't be the same as it was before he tied the knot with you.

Some widowers become very dependent on the late wife's family—especially if the widower has minor children still living at home. The in-laws may be full-time babysitters, help out the widower financially, or even invite him to live with them for a while. Other widowers get in the habit of eating Sunday dinner with the in-laws or spending every holiday with them. At some point, he's going to have to make a decision about whether he wants things to continue as they are, or to spend more of his life with you. If he's serious about tying the knot, it shouldn't be a hard decision.

After Krista died, the only in-laws I kept in touch with were her brother, Scott, and grandmother, Loretta. (I was never on good terms with Krista's parents.) Once I became seriously involved with Julianna, I kept Scott and Loretta posted on how things were progressing. As my new relationship became more serious, I spent less time with them. I was open about where my life was going, and they were accepting and understanding about the reason for the change, even if they both had a difficult time seeing me start a new life with someone else.

Scott was a good friend, in many ways like a brother

to me, but I understood that my relationship with my former in-laws had to change when I remarried. This wasn't because I didn't love him or care about him anymore, but because Julianna had to be my main focus.

After Julianna and I were married, I slowly lost touch with Scott. (Loretta passed away soon after.) We exchanged the occasional phone call and email and talked about getting together, but nothing ever happened. Then one day, after a long communication drought, I sent him an email. Much to my surprise, the email bounced back because the address had been closed. At that moment, I realized I had no way to contact him. Instead, my new marriage, moving fifty miles away, a new job, and children had all changed my life. Scott made decisions that changed his life too. The result of our decisions effectively broke the bond we used to have.

A widower's relationship with his in-laws usually doesn't deteriorate completely after a he remarries. But it does change. Widowers who have difficulty accepting changes to their relationship may not be ready to give their hearts to the new woman in their lives. Moving on means making the new woman number one in his heart and mind. If a widower is unwilling to alter the relationship with the in-laws, it could be a sign that he's not ready to start a new life with you.

You're Not Obligated to Spend Time with Them

If you feel uncomfortable spending time with the late wife's family, don't feel obligated to attend every activity or event. It's okay to let the widower and his kids spend some time alone with them. What you need to do is communicate why you feel this way—be sure he understands why you're staying home, and that you're supportive of the time he spends with them.

For example, Julianna never accompanied me to Scott or Loretta's home. This was not a specific request of hers, or because of anything Scott or Loretta did. Rather, it was a combination of general insecurities that came from feeling that Krista (via her family) was always going to play a part in our new life together. When we did spend time with Scott and Loretta, it was usually at church, neighborhood parties, or at my home. It wasn't the ideal solution for everyone, but it was one that worked for us.

Don't Be Afraid to Walk Away

If being involved with the late wife's family is a deal breaker, or you and the widower aren't able to come to an agreement on how much time you should spend with the former in-laws, end the relationship. There's no point in marrying someone if you can't accept or live with their past, and their other family members being part—even a small part—of your new life. At that point, it's simply better to cut your losses, move on, and start anew.

The moment I realized I was going to spend the rest of my life with Julianna, I reached a fork in the proverbial road of life. The one less traveled was the one Julianna and I would take together. The other was more worn and familiar, and it involved keeping my life and my relationships with my late wife's family as they were. It was impossible to travel both. I had a decision to make between my past life and a new one. I decided to travel the new road—which, as the saying goes, has made all the difference.

TAMI'S STORY

I was best friends with my husband's late wife from high school until her untimely death at the age of 26. She was that friend who was more like a sister, and her family always treated me as such. The family was crushed when they learned of her passing and relied heavily on my strength, as well as others', to help them through such a difficult time. I wrote a small speech for her wake and read it as her mother shakily clenched my left arm.

In the weeks following her death, her widowed husband and I kept in touch and became close friends. Soon we both felt an unexplainable desire to be part of each other's lives. Friendship turned to romance, romance turned to love, and here we are today, engaged to be married.

Her family wasn't thrilled that we had become a couple. They felt as if he was trying to replace her with me, that I was robbing him of his grief, and as if she was being pushed to a faraway place in our hearts and minds. This was not the case at all, since the widower and I talked often of her, her family, and our future together.

I felt a deep amount of guilt about being the reason behind their pain. One day I realized that they weren't mad at me. They were upset that she was gone and that their family and lives would never be the same without her. I had taken everything personally, when their feelings had nothing to with me or my relationship with the widower. Once I came to realize that the issue was with their own loss, things became clearer.

With this knowledge, the widower and I were able to have heart-to-heart talks with each member of her family about us, our relationship, and the late wife. This was a trying time for everyone involved. The former in-laws needed to realize that their former son-in-law was moving forward, making me number one in his heart, and that I was not trying to take her place or move in on a grieving man. We did not want to be the cause of any more pain, nor did we want to sacrifice our own desires to see this relationship flourish. Finally, after several months, they reached a point in which they embraced our love for each other and hoped that the two of us could be happy.

Now and in the future, they will continue to be a part of our lives, but not like before. Life changes in an instant, and while I'm still here, I'm going to make sure that my future husband and I can enjoy everything life has to offer, and that includes accepting that the late wife's family are a part of his past and mine. Transitions are not easy, but there usually is an up once you hit the bottom. As long as we keep our heads held high and our hearts in the right place, things will work out well for all parties involved. That, in my opinion, is all we can hope for.

VICKIE'S STORY

My husband's former mother-in-law passed away on New Year's Day. The morning of the viewing, I looked in the newspaper to read her obituary. To many people's surprise, but not to mine, after listing the names and spouses of her three surviving daughters, my husband and I were included as her son-in-law and his wife.

The funeral service was performed by one of her

sons-in-law. He spoke about the closeness of their family. He then told everyone how, when my husband and I became serious, there was a slight feeling of trepidation. How was this new person going to change the dynamics of the family? Could the inclusion of someone new drive a wedge into the family unit? He then explained that by accepting each other, and the mutual desire to maintain happiness and harmony, were mutually paramount. The two "mothers" set the standard for the entire family. It was important to both of us to get along. We were lucky that we liked each other from the start.

I understand that our relationship could have gone in the opposite direction. I could have wanted *nothing* to do with her family. They could have had hurt feelings and not accepted me or anyone else. But everything worked out. I didn't fight or complain about everything they said or did, and they didn't become upset when I changed the decor of the house and asked them to take whatever of her belongings they wanted. We tried to be mindful of each other's feelings and hope that everything would work out for the best.

No, the late wife's mom did not become like another

mother to me. Her daughters did not become my new best friends. I did, however, *want* to invite them to our wedding, and they joyfully attended. I look forward to spending every Christmas Eve with them. I enjoy having them stay in my home when they come to visit their niece. In fact, I told my husband before he even asked that *yes*, if his newly widowed first father-in-law would like to come stay with us for a while, he's more than welcome.

My husband and I will celebrate our seventh wedding anniversary this summer. *Her* family has been a part of my life for nearly nine years. In fact, they are *my* family. I would have to say that we all made a conscious decision from the beginning not to be mean or petty or hurt about the situation. I have heard so many stories about toxic former in-laws. I am so relieved to have the in-laws I do. (Yes, I consider them in-laws). I am extremely blessed in this situation, and I am truly aware of it.

You can't expect someone to erase people from his/her life just because someone died. My husband is extremely close to his late wife's family. Because of my love for him and his daughter, I wanted to accept the in-laws into my life. I imagine they all felt the same way about accepting me. I kept my mouth shut at some things, and I suppose they did too. Knowing there were no ill feelings made our blending possible. Life is tough already. Why make it tougher?

CHAPTER 4

MAKING A HOME TOGETHER

HOMES ARE POWERFUL THINGS. From birthdays to holidays to other special moments, homes are places where many great memories are created. They reflect the tastes of its inhabitants, and in a sense, become extensions of the people who live there. Marrying a widower often means moving into the home he and the late wife shared. Ideally, it would be nice to make a clean start together and create your own memories. If possible, this is the path I encourage, as a new home can make it mentally and emotionally easier for everyone to start over.

That being said, it's not always possible to get a new place. At times, because of employment, children still living at home, or finances, it simply makes more sense to live in the home that the widower and his late wife shared. This means that even if her photos are taken down (which they should be) and her clothes and other personal belongings are all given away or boxed up somewhere (as they should be too), her dishes are still in the cupboard, her paint or wallpaper is on the walls, and her carpet is on the floor. Living in a home that's largely unchanged can make it harder for widowers to move on, because their surroundings reflect the late wife. Redecorating the house to some degree isn't just for your sanity, but to give the widower a sense that he really is starting a new chapter in his life.

If the two of you decide that living in his home is the best option, you need to decide what you can change about it and what will remain the same. Determine exactly what it will take to make you feel more comfortable living there. The last thing you want is to feel trapped in a home that reeks of the past. The changes don't have to be dramatic. They could be as simple as new paint or wallpaper, or different carpet and a few pieces of furniture.

Once you figure out what it will take, talk to the

widower about making changes. Most widowers haven't given a second thought to what the inside of the house looks like. Odds are, his late wife did the house the way she wanted, and he just went along with it. When you bring up the subject of redecorating, remember not to trash the late wife's tastes, no matter how different or tacky they may seem. Putting down the late wife is the fastest way to get a resounding "No!" to all of your suggestions. Instead, keep the conversation focused on what you can do to make the home a place you both like. Together, figure out what you can do to make things work, and agree on a budget for it. No matter how much or little you have to spend, in the end, the home should be a place where everyone who lives there can feel welcome and comfortable.

Don't feel like you have to get rid of everything. There may be some things you want to keep. One woman mentioned in an email that the late wife had a killer set of cookware that she was never, ever going to part with. Make a list and decide what absolutely has to go (or be packed up) and what things can stay. If you have belongings of your own, you may not be able to put everything of yours in your new home. You'll have to prioritize those as well. Then talk to the widower about changes he'd like to see and, if you don't see eye-to-eye on those changes, come up with something that will make you both happy. Keep in mind that unless he has gobs of money lying around, you may not be able to redo the entire house. Instead, you might have to pick some things on the list and save others for later. Maybe there are one or two things the widower will want to keep as-is. Work out a plan so that whatever you do, the widower is aware of the changes and that you both feel comfortable with the final result. Remember—the purpose of redecorating is to make you both feel good about your new start.

The widower may want to hold on to certain household items for sentimental or practical reasons. You may have compromise some here, so long as they aren't items that make you feel like you're living with a ghost.

When Julianna and I started dating, I lived in a home I bought soon after Krista's death. Even though we had never lived there together, it was the house Krista had always wanted us to buy and remodel. After Julianna and I became engaged, we talked about where we were going to live. Initially, we talked about living in my house. Julianna was open to the idea so long as she could make some changes. The place looked more like a bachelor pad than an actual residence, but even so, Julianna couldn't live with the few things of Krista's that were still there. I was fine with her making changes, provided that some items could simply be stored away in the basement.

The more I thought about it, the more I felt I should sell the house so Julianna and I could start our new life together in a place where we wouldn't be held back by the past. Looking back nine years later, it was the right decision for us. Even though we moved again a year after we were married, every time we drive by the town where we first lived, we can talk about memories special for the two of us. In addition, living in a new town forced us to make new friends and helped us both rely a little more on each other than we would have otherwise. The move brought us closer in ways that living in my house never could have.

When Julianna and I moved, things from my past life came with us—a kitchen table and chairs, a chest of drawers, some blankets, a television, books, and other miscellaneous items. Keep in mind that we were both in our twenties and just starting out in life, so neither of us had a lot. The kitchen table may not have been to Julianna's liking, but it was better than the one she had. It served us well for many years before we finally upgraded to something else. Even now, when I walk through our current house, I see a few things here and there from my first marriage. Some of them may be replaced in the coming years, while others may stay with us until one, or both of us, passes on. No matter how much or little remains of my past life, Julianna has a home she can feel comfortable in, and we both have a home that feels like ours. You should feel the same way.

For the sake of your marriage and your sanity, do what's necessary to make the house a place where the two of you can spend the rest of your lives. Whether it's a new home or just redoing the old one, make it a place where you can both create new memories and a loving environment. Sometimes we have to do everything we can to start a new life together. And if that means making the house seem new again, so be it.

CHAPTER 5

STARTING A
NEW LIFE TOGETHER

PEOPLE ARE CREATURES of habit. The longer we perform a routine or engage in certain behaviors, the harder they become to change. Widowers are no different. For years, they've become accustomed to doing things a certain way with the late wife, and often those habits and traditions carry over into their new relationship.

For example, some women who are in serious relationships with a widower eat at the same restaurants, pray at the same churches or synagogues, party with the same friends, and even vacation at the same places he and the late wife enjoyed. Instead of feeling like they're starting a new life, the woman comes to think of the relationship as a rehash of his first marriage. It grows old very quickly and drives them crazy.

To be fair, most men aren't trying to relive the past. They're just used to living their life a certain way and want to continue doing the same things after they've fallen in love with someone else. Often they're blind to how visiting the same places or involving you in activities that he and the late wife enjoyed make you feel. They're simply living their life as they've done for years—only with you by their side.

When Julianna and I started dating, I took her to many of the same restaurants and museums Krista and I had frequented. I didn't do this to relive the good times Krista and I shared or because I was hoping Julianna would like the same things Krista had. I just knew those were places where the food would be delicious, or where I knew we would enjoy our time together. I was also new to the dating game, and many times it seemed as if our relationship was this close to crumbling if something else went wrong. The last thing I wanted to do was try a place that might result in a bad night out together.

Admittedly, it felt weird the first few times I took Julianna to places where Krista and I had gone. Sometimes it was downright surreal to be in the same place, surrounded by so many memories of doing similar things with Krista. That didn't stop me from enjoying my time with Julianna, but it was distracting. As our relationship grew stronger and we grew together, I got more adventurous and started trying new places.

Even if the widower's intentions are innocent, doing the same things he and the late wife did isn't good for your marriage in the long run. Your relationship will be a lot stronger when you both explore new places and do things that will create memories as something just the two of you can share.

Some of the memories Julianna and I have created over the last nine years are vacations to Seattle, Idaho, Phoenix, Las Vegas, Houston, and Denver. We've gone to baseball games, museums, and national parks that neither of us visited before we met. We've blended and instituted new Christmas and other holiday traditions to make those times feel like our own special occasions. As a result, we have memories and experiences unique to us. These have helped cement our relationship into something strong and unbreakable. Each year, we do things we haven't done before. It's been a fun challenge to come up with something new to try. If you or your widower aren't this adventurous, at least try to find one trip destination or tradition you can incorporate into your new marriage. Even that one trip or tradition, done once a year, will go a long way toward helping you start a new life together.

Not all widowers have an easy time with change. Even if they're ready to move on, they may have a hard time giving up habits that have been part of their lives for years. If your widower is struggling with trying something new, instead of complaining, suggest two or three other places you can both enjoy. A widower who has embraced you as number one will be open to doing and trying new things with you and creating new memories. In fact, he may have suggestions—be open to his ideas too. Together, you should be able to find a way to make new memories that the two of you can treasure for the rest of your lives. Widowers who truly love you will be sensitive to your feelings and do their best to create new memories with you—even if it's difficult for them.

STARTING NEW TRADITIONS

Building a life together is more than just going out and trying new things or visiting new places. It's also about starting new traditions at home and during the holidays. It's about doing things that make you both feel like you're starting something new. They don't have to be new traditions, but they can be a blending or altering of family traditions the two of you already have.

Julianna and I didn't want to do the same things we'd done in previous relationships. We adapted things as necessary to create new traditions as part of our relationship. For example, when we were dating and newly married, we went running together every morning. We took our common interest and started something we could both enjoy. As kids came along, we altered the activity to family runs when the weather was warm, but again, we tried to do things we could both enjoy. For Christmas traditions, we borrowed heavily from things Julianna had done as a kid and some things I had done, and adapted them. In the end, we had something to share with our kids that was unique to our family.

Another fun tradition I started when we got married is making elaborate breakfasts on Sunday mornings. It's something the kids look forward to as well.

If you marry a widower with minor children living at home, changing traditions or eliminating them outright probably isn't a good idea, as they may be having a hard time adjusting to their new life. What you can do is alter existing traditions somewhat, or include some of your own.

For example, one lady was dreading the upcoming Christmas season. She had married a widower with three children still living at home. It had been a family tradition on the Sunday after Thanksgiving to unpack the ornaments and decorate the house. All the decorations in the home were the late wife's. The new wife didn't know if she could get through the holiday season if she had to endure looking at the late wife's Christmas touches all over the home.

She was still sensitive to the needs of the widower's children and was worried that a flood of new ornaments would upset them—especially a teenage daughter still having trouble with the fact that her father had remarried. In the end, they were able to come to a compromise where the kids picked out and kept the ornaments that meant the most to them, while she bought a bunch of new ones that could make her feel as though she belonged in the family.

Whatever you do, don't let your marriage get stuck in the traditions of the past. Go out, make new friends, and try new things together. These activities can help elevate and invigorate a new relationship. You may not be able to start from scratch, but you can start in a way that will give the relationship a freshness that will bring you both closer together.

CATHY'S STORY

The first weekend getaway Ben and I took together was to San Diego. We stayed in a nice hotel, ate at nice restaurants, attended a baseball game, and had a wonderful time together. It wasn't until our drive home that he told me that San Diego was a trip he and his late wife had made every year for the last two decades. To make bad news worse, I also learned that the hotel we stayed at and most of the places we ate were the same places *they* enjoyed when they were married. At first, the news made me sick to my stomach, but Ben assured me that he was ready to move on. I thought for a long moment and thought he deserved a second chance.

The next week, we were eating at a restaurant he suggested, and I found out that it was a place he and the late wife frequented. I had the same sick feeling in my stomach and was unable to finish my meal. Ben said that he brought me there because the food was good, not because it was a place that he and the late wife liked. I decided to give Ben another chance.

For nearly two years, our relationship was one of second, third, and fourth chances. Nearly everything we did—from vacations to eating out to recreational activities and the shows we watched on TV—were things that *they* had enjoyed. It was rare that the widower would leave his comfort zone, and when he did, he always found something to complain about.

I felt like I was trapped in the marriage of Ben and his late wife. I kept telling myself that things would get better if he just had more time to grieve, but they never did. Ironically, it was when Ben asked me to marry him that I realized I couldn't spend the rest of my life with someone who wasn't willing to make the necessary adjustments to make our relationship special. I packed up my things that night and never looked back.

My problem was that I kept making excuses for Ben's behavior. I rarely stood up for myself, and I rationalized away the red flags that kept popping up. Please don't ever do this. Be strong and stand up for yourself. If you see red flags, don't be afraid to put your foot down and let him know that he has to make you number one. My relationship with Ben taught me a lot of lessons that I had to learn the hard way. I hope that other women who read this learn from my mistakes and don't repeat them. You're unique and exceptional. Don't let a widower treat you like anything less.

CHAPTER 6

PARENTING AND BLENDING FAMILIES

NOTE: *This chapter focuses on parenting minor children (ages 17 and under) who still live with you or the widower. If you want tips and tricks for dealing with adult children, refer to Chapter 4 of* Dating a Widower.

THIS CHAPTER won't tell you how to raise your kids or the widower's children. There are lots of different parenting philosophies out there, and how to bring up your kids is something the two of you need to agree on *before* you tie the knot. What I will do is give you some general guidance for how you and the widower can work together to make the transition of blending families, or becoming first-time parents, easier.

As the father of five, I know that parenting is a tough,

but ultimately rewarding, job. If you're a parent, you know that too. But whether you're going to become an instant mom or dad, or you're both bringing kids into the marriage, here are five simple things that can make the transition of starting a new family together less stressful, and, hopefully, more successful.

Put Each Other First

Widowers who say that their children come first have no business remarrying. For any marriage to succeed, you both need to make each other the top priority in your life. This doesn't mean neglecting any children in the relationship, or that you stop taking care of them when it becomes inconvenient. Rather, it means doing what it takes to keep your marriage functional and your relationship strong. Besides, if you're not willing to play second fiddle to the late wife, you shouldn't be willing to come in second to his children, either.

Even though our five children are very important to me and Julianna, we don't have a problem putting off a meal for fifteen minutes so we can go have a discussion instead of arguing or discussing sensitive matters in front of the kids. We scrimp and save money for a babysitter so we can have an evening all to ourselves once or twice a month. We do what it takes to let each other know that we value our marriage, and we do our best to keep it strong. Our basic obligations to our children are to give them food and shelter, to teach them right from wrong, and to provide a loving home for them. One day they'll leave the nest and start families of their own. Once they're gone, all we'll have is each other, and if we don't have a strong relationship, odds are we won't even make it that far.

BE ON THE SAME PAGE WHEN IT COMES TO PARENTING

Not everyone has the same parenting philosophy. Even in marriage, parents can have different ideas on the best way to raise or discipline children. As husband and wife, you're raising your children together. That involves making decisions based on what's good for individual family members and the family as a whole. It's hard to do that if you're not working as a team.

That doesn't mean you have to agree on every little aspect of parenting, but it does mean that you need to talk things over, negotiate if necessary, and figure out a way to provide a united front. It's vital that you figure out these issues before you get married. Talk about them beforehand and continue to refine your approach as needed.

Pay attention to how the widower parents his children and decide if you're comfortable with the approach. If you have kids of your own, would you be okay if they were treated in a similar manner? If not, what would you do differently?

You're a Parent First and Foremost

One of the more difficult aspects of marrying a widower with children is becoming an instant mother to kids who may not be thrilled that their father is remarrying. As a result, it's natural for some women to try making friends with the widower's children, hoping it will help the children become more accepting of you. While it's a good thing to build a relationship of trust with the widower's children, don't make the mistake of becoming their friend instead of their parent. Being a parent—even a stepparent—means you're the boss. That means they need to be able to count on you and the widower as the ones who make decisions and run the show. As a parent, you're a protector, educator, guide, helper, supporter, motivator, disciplinarian, consultant, advisor, and nurturer, as well as many other things. Being a friend, however, is not one of them.

Being a parent means you're going to have to make some hard calls that the kids are going to find unpopular. They may scream that you aren't their real mom or that they wish their mom hadn't died. Don't take these comments personally—and still be the mom.

Have Each Other's Back

Some children have a problem when Mom or Dad decides to start dating again—let alone remarry. In the case of losing a parent, it could mean they're still grieving, or they're simply having a hard time seeing Dad with someone else. Unfortunately, sometimes they feel they can treat you not as a parent, but as trash. It's important that the widower stand up to his children to lovingly defend you if they're pushing back. Maybe that means having a chat with the kids to explain how things are going to work from now on.

If the widower can't, or is unwilling, to defend you to his children, think twice about the relationship, because you're in for a long and miserable marriage even after his children leave the home. If he can't honor you now, odds are he's not going to do it after you're married.

～～～

RITA'S STORY

When my fiancé asked me to marry him, he came bearing gifts. In addition to the beautiful sapphire ring he gave me, he also brought his two-year-old daughter, Emma, into our relationship. I had a seven-year-old daughter from a previous relationship. In our choosing to marry each other, our little girls were becoming sisters.

In the beginning there were many questions: Would I formally adopt Emma? Would our girls be able to bond together? Would Emma and I have the same mother/child bond that my biological daughter and I shared? Would other people accept me as

Emma's mother? Would she call me "Mommy?" What if I did things differently than his late wife did? Would I be judged?

Most of the questions worked themselves out easily and early on. Yes, we would adopt, formally. Yes, our girls were able to bond together (we like to say they *really* are sisters now every time we hear them engaged in a healthy debate). Yes, I bonded easily with Emma, and she has called me Mommy on her own, practically from the beginning.

Despite us coming together in all of these things, one area was particularly challenging for us: Emma's maternal grandmother refused to accept me as Emma's mother. It was a stressful time. Because it was difficult for Grandma to hear Emma call me "Mommy," she chose to not acknowledge me and only wished to see my husband by himself. Also, because she had been the caretaker of both my husband and her grandchild after her daughter passed away, it wasn't as easy for her to move forward. In her mind, she was losing both her son-in-law and granddaughter to someone else.

I tried to be sensitive to her feelings as we all adjusted to the new situation, though that didn't make it easier for me to send Emma to stay with her grand-mother for once-monthly visitations. I was worried sick that Grandma would tell my child that I was not her real mother, or that she'd project her sadness and grief onto this young toddler. My gut reaction was to respond harshly and refuse visitation until she could see things the way I did. But deep down I knew that wasn't the right thing to do. I knew any words ex-changed between us early on could shape and damage our long-term relationship. Instead, my husband and I continued to approach the situation with love and patience.

Emma still went to visit her grandmother, and my husband communicated effectively with his former mother-in-law on my behalf. We set and respected boundaries, and we asked that her grief not be used as an excuse to treat me poorly. Over time, I am happy to say, the situation vastly improved. It is not perfect, and I don't know if Emma's grandmother will ever think of me as Emma's mother. But she has accepted our marriage as fact and doesn't appear to tell Emma otherwise.

I am happy to report that our family has bonded

more closely because of the adversities we faced early in our marriage. Those challenges were an opportunity to set important boundaries and hone important communication skills which will serve as a lasting foundation. The truth is, Emma has two mothers: the one who birthed her, and the one who will raise her. And while that was difficult for some to accept, it is a wonderful truth for our little girl. When I look at our family, I do not feel that we are different from any other family out there. We stand on our love. And sometimes that (with time and patience) is enough to carry you through.

CHAPTER 7

WHERE TO BURY THE SECOND WIFE
(AND WHAT TO DO WITH THE ASHES OF THE FIRST ONE)

MARRIAGE IS THE CELEBRATION of two people staring a new life together. Ironically, concerns like where the two of you will be buried and what to do with the ashes of the late wife can end the relationship before either one of you have said "I do." While there are some death-related issues—like what to do with the remains of the late wife—that you need to resolve or figure out before tying the knot, some subjects, like where the two of you should be laid to rest, shouldn't concern you if you can't come to an agreement.

WHERE SHOULD YOU BE BURIED?

In our nine years as husband and wife, there is only one widower-related issue Julianna and I have been unable to agree on: where we should be laid to rest after one of us dies. Although we both want to be buried next to each other, I want to be buried between her and my late wife. Julianna prefers for the two of us to be buried elsewhere.

The subject came up sometime between our engagement and marriage. I was kind of surprised that she wasn't happy with what I thought was an ideal arrangement. After all, it seemed reasonable for the three of us to be buried side-by-side—especially since I already have a plot for myself next to Krista, and my family has a plot next to mine. There's plenty of room for Julianna and any of our children who may want to be laid to rest there, but she doesn't see it that way. She wants us to be buried next to each other somewhere else.

We went back and forth over this for a week or so and were unable to resolve the issue. It came up occasionally in the first few years we were married, but we didn't come to any kind of agreement or compromise.

In the end, we decided it wasn't worth arguing about. After all, cemeteries and burial plots are for the living. The dead have other concerns. We decided that whoever is the last one standing can bury the other person wherever they want. It may not be the perfect solution, but it's one we can both live with, and it helps us focus our energy and attention on our marriage and the present.

If you can't agree on where the two of you should be buried, don't let it ruin your relationship. In the big picture, where one's body is laid to rest isn't that important. Instead, spend time and energy strengthening the love you have now. Life is short, and it can end in an instant. Pick your battles wisely. Unless there is an absolutely compelling reason to decide now, put the issue to the side and concentrate on each other with the time you're able to spend together.

DOUBLE HEADSTONES

Widowers who choose to bury the late wife, instead of cremating her remains, sometimes purchase a double headstone with her name on it and a spot for his once he passes on. This can cause contention and hurt feelings, because it can make the new woman feel like the widower's heart still belongs to the late wife.

If your widower bought a double headstone before you started dating, don't take it personally or as a sign that he loves the late wife more than you. Odds are, it was purchased soon after the late wife's burial. At the time, dating again—let alone remarrying—were the last things on his mind.

A few months after Krista died, I bought a double headstone. Instead of my name, I chose to have the name of our late daughter, Hope, inscribed on it, since she's buried with her mother. But even if I had left a space for my name, it wouldn't have been done with the intention of spiting a future wife. I bought what seemed right at the time. Odds are, your widower felt the same way when he purchased the headstone for his late wife as well.

THE LATE WIFE'S ASHES

Moving on isn't just a mental and emotional process; it's a physical one as well. We have funerals and memorial services or scatter ashes so we can go through the physical act of saying good-bye to someone. Attending a funeral or some other service is something most people need to experience before they can start a journey of mentally and emotionally grieving and moving on.

When the deceased wife is cremated, sometimes the widower doesn't scatter her ashes. Instead, he'll keep them in an urn on display in the home. This isn't a problem, unless he's looking to remarry. Once he's decided to start a new life with someone, the ashes have to go. This is one issue you can't put off until after you're married. Don't marry a widower who refuses to move the late wife's ashes.

Having the ashes around is just like having a hundred large, framed photographs of the late wife covering every inch of the house. If he's serious about moving on, her ashes need to be scattered according to her wishes, given to someone else for safe keeping, or stored in a place where they'll never be disturbed for the rest of your marriage. A widower unable to remove ashes from his home will never be able to make room in his heart for his new wife.

If the deceased didn't give any directions for what to do with her remains, then the widower needs to figure out the best way to say goodbye. He can scatter her ashes at a special location, split them up between family members, have them interred at a cemetery, or pack them away, so long as you don't have to worry about them. Putting the ashes away shouldn't be a hard thing to do if the widower is actually ready to start a new life with you.

～～～

LAURIE'S STORY

John, his late wife, and I were lifelong friends. Soon after his wife died, he sold his home and moved into a townhouse. The first time I visited John's new place, I was struck by the excessive number of photographs lining the entry wall from the top of a credenza to the ceiling. And on top of the credenza was the cardboard box containing John's wife's ashes.

That same evening, I asked John what he planned to do with the ashes. Even though six weeks had passed since her death, I thought perhaps he had a memorial service in mind, and I wanted to attend. He said his wife's wish was to have them scattered in the ocean, in a location where she'd spent a lot of time as a young girl. I asked when he planned to do this, and he responded that he wasn't ready.

Over the next two-and-a-half months, I visited him occasionally and asked whether he'd given any thought to scattering her ashes. Eventually, he said he thought he'd invite a handful of school friends they'd grown up with to have dinner on the Gulf Coast, and afterward, they'd walk out on the pier for a brief memorial service and scatter her ashes. I gently nudged him to do this sooner than later. Again, he responded that he wasn't ready.

Then one evening, I walked into his home and noticed that all of the photographs of his wife had been removed from the wall, but the ashes were still there. I took this as the first step toward him moving forward with his life.

Within a week, John made a surprising declaration: he thought he should be married to me. Even though I thought I wanted to be married to him, I said an emphatic *No,* and suggested he wasn't ready to be married again as long as he was unwilling to dispose of his wife's ashes. He said he'd do it soon, that he just needed a little more time. How *much* time was his decision to make. Only John could decide what felt right. And I didn't want to be blamed down the line for rushing him into tending to this matter sooner than he was inclined to take care of it on his own. But I did suggest that he needed to scatter her ashes before we could move forward as a couple.

Several days after John had a chance to marinate in that thought, I said yes to the idea of marriage. He pressed me for a wedding date, stating, "I'd marry you right now!" I told him I didn't want to commit to a specific date until he disposed of his wife's ashes. To me, hanging on to them was tantamount to having a dead body around the house. This time, John stayed mute on the subject. I didn't know if he was planning to find a way to keep the ashes, or merely thoughtfully considering his options.

When the issue of where we would live came up, we agreed that the logical thing to do was to move into my house, since John was living in a rental property. He again pressed me for a wedding date. Again,

I mentioned that if he wasn't prepared to scatter her ashes, then maybe he was moving too fast, and we shouldn't get married until that was done. He asked why it couldn't be done later, after we were married, and I had to tell him what I'd been thinking since the day he asked me to marry him—*because you're not moving her ashes into my house.*

A few weeks later, he set a date on his own for his wife's memorial. He invited me to accompany him on the six-hour drive and to attend the dinner and memorial, but I declined. I felt it would be inappropriate to travel that far with him, attend such a service, and stay overnight, even though I knew all the people who would be attending. I did feel bad that he'd have to do this on his own, but it was the only way I could ensure that this was a move he'd elected to do, and not a move he was forced to do. It also gave him the time and space to grieve with the friends they'd grown up with, without distraction.

When John returned from the memorial for his wife, he seemed relieved, and almost content that he'd carried out her last request. He described the journey, the conversations with their friends, and the memorial service, and it seemed both meaningful and done in good taste.

We married six months later.

CHAPTER 8

SETTING EXPECTATIONS: YOU'RE NOT THE LATE WIFE!

ONE OF THE BIGGEST CHANGES widowers have to make when preparing to tie the knot again is adjusting to the new wife's personality and her unique way of doing things. Even though I loved Julianna immensely and treated her as the center of my universe, after we married, there were still times when I had to remember that Julianna wasn't Krista.

For example, one of the things Krista and I loved to eat was a pizza covered in sausage, mushrooms, and olives. Soon after Julianna and I were married, I bought the same pizza, thinking that she would like it just as much as Krista had—forgetting, of course, that

Julianna doesn't like mushrooms or olives. One of the first gifts I bought Julianna was a nice hardback notebook to use as a journal. I thought she'd like writing in one just as much as Krista had. I forgot she wasn't a writer and had little interest in keeping a journal. Julianna also has different tastes in jewelry. She likes silver things: rings, earrings, and necklaces. Krista preferred gold. Even though I knew this, the first piece of jewelry I bought Julianna was—you guessed it—gold.

Adjusting to life with Julianna was more than just realizing her likes and tastes. There were personality issues as well. For example, Julianna's a lot quieter and more thoughtful than Krista. Krista never had a problem telling me how she felt about things, while Julianna was much more reserved. Though she didn't have a hard time expressing her feelings, she often needed time to think about what she was going to say. When we were first married, the fact that she wasn't as loud and boisterous drove me crazy. It took a while for me to realize that just because she didn't speak out as often or needed time to formulate her thoughts, didn't mean that I had hurt her feelings or that she was angry or upset with me. The first few months of our marriage, it felt like I was constantly trying to figure out how she was feeling and what she was thinking. I finally made the adjustment, but it took a lot of mental fine-tuning in order for me to realize that Julianna was a unique person with her own habits and quirks.

The adjustment period wasn't just difficult for me. It was also difficult for Julianna. At times she interpreted my words and actions to mean that I wanted her to be more like Krista. Other times, she thought I wished I were still *with* Krista. I never felt that way, but sometimes when something didn't go according to plan, she felt that way. While there's nothing you can do about the differences between you and the late wife (nor should you try), the key is learning how to react to the widower during this adjustment phase.

Don't Take It Personally

Odds are, the widower isn't trying to mold you into the late wife when he says or implies that he likes things done a certain way. He's probably just reverting back to his old habits, so don't worry that he doesn't love you or that he wishes the late wife was still around. It takes time to adjust to new ideas and ways of doing things. See if the widower is actually trying to make the necessary changes and adjustments to you and the new relationship.

BE FLEXIBLE

You have your own unique personality and way of doing things, but marriage is about adjusting, changing, and knowing when to compromise. For example, say the late wife liked to cook and was really good at whipping up fabulous dishes on the fly. During the course of their marriage, the widower became accustomed to having nice, homemade meals most of the time. You know you don't have the same culinary skills—but so what? Maybe you can't make chicken à la king, but why not learn how to cook one or two dishes that you can make for him on special occasions? They don't have to be the same things the late wife cooked, but something else the two of you can enjoy together.

The widower should show the same ability to compromise as well. For example, I wasn't much of a cologne man when I married Krista. She never really cared if I wore any. But Julianna likes it when I put some on in the mornings or when we're going out. She found one she liked and asked me to try it. I liked it as well, and now, most mornings I'll put some on. At first, I did it because it was something she liked, but now I put some on because I enjoy it too.

BE YOURSELF

You need to feel comfortable being yourself around the widower, knowing he'll accept you for who you are—not because you remind him of the late wife. If you don't feel like you can be yourself at all times, that's a problem. You shouldn't hide part of yourself or your personality in order to make him happy. Men who truly love a woman will embrace everything about her. Widowers who love you and are ready to start a new life will make the necessary adjustments—even if it takes a little work—so you feel accepted and loved for who you are.

LET THE WIDOWER KNOW WHAT YOU LIKE

Widowers aren't mind readers. When you say you like flowers, he may show up with roses, when what you really wanted was a mixed bouquet. To help him avoid turning a kind gesture into an awkward moment, point out things that you like when opportunities present themselves. This can help the widower make the transition and be more sensitive to things you prefer.

I've improved quite a bit in the nine years since Julianna and I became husband and wife. I don't make most of the same boneheaded mistakes I made when we were first married. Julianna was patient with me, and I slowly became better at realizing and appreciating her likes and dislikes—it's not even an issue anymore. As long as you're patient and help educate the widower on who you are and what you like, you should see similar results.

EMILY'S STORY

The first time Jack gave me flowers, I almost cried. The flowers were a bouquet of pink lilies. They were beautiful, but they also happened to be the late wife's favorite flowers. It was all I could do not to burst into tears when he handed them to me.

Jack could sense something was wrong. He asked me what it was, but I couldn't tell him. I was too hurt and couldn't bring myself to talk about it right then. Instead, I abruptly ended our date and went home, where I promptly threw the flowers in the trash, followed by a good cry before I went to bed.

The next morning, I got up and saw the tops of the wilting lilies sticking out of the trash can. As I started to close the lid so I wouldn't have to look at them, I had a sudden realization. Jack had been married to his late wife for 26 years, and, less than two years after her death, I was his first serious relationship. He wasn't trying to hurt me with the flowers. He had no idea what kind of flowers I liked. He was just trying to do something to show how much he loved me.

I immediately picked up the phone, called Jack, and told him we needed to talk. That afternoon we met for coffee. After some small talk, I explained why the flowers had upset me. He started to apologize, but I told him that I was in the wrong. I had taken offense at his lovely gift when none was meant, and I had no reason to act the way I did. I asked him if he could forgive me for my rash judgment, and if we could start anew.

We did, and a year later, we were married.

As I write this, Jack and I have been married three years. It hasn't always been smooth sailing. There were other times while we were dating when Jack did something or gave me a gift because that's what the late wife would have liked. When those moments happened, I smiled and reminded Jack who I am and what I like. Despite these little setbacks, he's *always* made a good effort to adjust to my wants and likes, and I've done my best to make sure to keep his wants and likes in the forefront of my mind too.

Ironically, I don't think we would ever have gotten married if it hadn't been for that bouquet of pink lilies. It taught us both that we were starting a new life together and would have to be patient with each other as we learned the ropes and how to make each other number one. Now when a pink lily happens to catch my eye, I think of how lucky I am to be married to a man who was willing to give me a second chance.

CHAPTER 9

ARE YOU READY TO MARRY A WIDOWER?

WAS THE LATE WIFE prettier than you? Was she smarter? A better lover? A better cook? Did she understand the widower better than you ever will? Do you think there's no way you'll ever be able to measure up to her?

At some point, just about everyone who's considering marrying a widower goes through a phase where they feel that the late wife did everything right, and no matter how hard they try, they'll never be as good or as smart or as attractive as she was. Julianna worried about how she'd compare in the bedroom, whether or not I'd tire of her quiet personality, or whether she'd be as good as cook as Krista. Krista was a good person and a great wife, but she wasn't a saint; she had flaws and made mistakes just like anyone else. The late wife of the widower you're dating is no different. When someone dies, people tend to remember the good things about them, and not the bad.

Comparing yourself to the late wife is only going to make you feel insecure and cause you to second-guess yourself. The truth is, widowers who choose to remarry do it because they've found someone else who can make their hearts flutter with excitement every time she walks into a room. You need to remember that he loves you for who you are, *not* because you remind him of someone else. Expressing doubt about yourself will only make you less attractive to the widower.

Julianna has a quiet personality, is very detail-oriented, runs marathons, and has a bachelor's degree in chemistry. My late wife was talkative, let details slide, had no interest in exercising, and had a bachelor's degree in English. I could spend the next several pages detailing every little difference between the two, but in the end, none of that mattered. I didn't marry Julianna because she reminded me of Krista. I married her because I fell in love with the unique individual she is.

Next time you compare yourself to the late wife, figure out where it's coming from. Is it something the widower said or did, or is it because of your own internal insecurities? If the widower is constantly comparing the two of you through his words or actions, there's a big problem that needs to be fixed before you even consider exchanging rings. If you think you'll never live up to the romanticized image of the late wife, you need to stop those kinds of thoughts immediately. Little things are going to come up from time to time in your marriage, and if you don't get control of your feelings now, those things are really going to rip you apart.

Some junk mail might arrive addressed to her, an old photo may fall out of a book, or a friend might post a photo on the widower's Facebook page. You've got to brush these little things out of your mind and move on with life. They aren't important. What *is* important is that the widower treats you like the only woman he's ever loved.

At some point, you're going to have to put your insecurities to the side and take that leap of faith. Accept that he was married before and that it helped make him the man you know and love today. If the insecurities don't stop, or you're bothered to no end by the way the late wife keeps coming up, you need to stop and decide if you're really ready to say "I do."

∽

KAREN'S STORY

Compared to some women who date and marry widowers, I've had it pretty easy.

Within the first six months of our courtship, my guy put away the pictures of the late wife, as well as dealing with a couple of other bothersome widower issues, and convinced me that I held the number one spot in his heart.

Here was a widower who was ready to start a new life with a new person.

But was I? Was I ready to marry a widower?

This was the question I asked myself when my guy proposed.

Our progression from dating to cohabitation to marriage spanned about three years, so there was plenty of time to come to grips with the *widower realities* that remained after his fairly few and benign *widower issues* had been put to bed.

For example, my husband's late wife comes up in conversation from time to time, and I occasionally come upon her personal belongings. Years after her death, my husband is still shuffling through insurance bills from her long and complicated illness. Catalogs and other pieces of mail arrive with her name on them. There is a gravestone inscribed with both her name and his.

I pored through the entire inventory of these widower realities with soul-scraping honesty and realized I could live with them just fine. Either these things had ceased to spook me the way they used to, or they had never yanked my chain to begin with.

But there was more to the question—was I ready to marry a widower?

My husband cared deeply for his first wife, so I knew I was never going to be his one and only true love. Could I be happy as the true love of *this* chapter in his life?

Was I ready to stop making comparisons between myself and the late wife, between our marriage and theirs—comparisons that my husband and his family would never dream of making?

Was I ready to put his widowerhood in perspective, as a significant part of his past, but not the thing that defined him, or our relationship?

These were *my* widower issues, not his.

Luckily, all I had to do to resolve them was this: Stop thinking about the questions and start appreciating the fact that this man was already giving me more than I could ever ask for in a future spouse.

Now that we are married, my guy continues to be the whole enchilada, and then some.

Every day, he offers me affection, loyalty, friendship, and romance. He also provides me with daily doses of humor, intelligence, and fun. And on really good days, he spoils me with his tasty fried chicken.

Like I said, I've had it pretty easy.

CHAPTER 10

SIX OTHER THINGS TO THINK ABOUT

IT'S EASY to get so consumed wondering if the widower is ready to move on that you overlook other issues vital to a successful relationship. While making sure he's ready to start a new life with you is extremely important, widower-related issues tend to fade into the background the longer you've been married, and other personality issues take the forefront. That's why the last chapter of this book has *nothing* to do with whether or not a widower is ready to move on. Instead, it's going to focus on six other important areas you need to consider before exchanging vows. At the very least, this chapter is a chance for you to take some time to think about your relationship and decide whether the man you're dating is really someone you can be with for the rest of your life.

I came up with these six areas one day while wondering how I could fall in love with two people who seemed, at least on the outside, to be the exact opposite of each other. It wasn't until Julianna and I had been married for several years that I realized both Julianna and Krista share a core of common beliefs and values that are exactly the same. I've talked to widows and widowers who have had successful second marriages, and most of them agree that their late spouses and their second spouses matched up well in at least five of the six areas.

My personal opinion is that you need to match up in at least five of these six areas to have a good chance of a successful marriage. If you have fewer than five points, there's going to be a lot more stress in the relationship.

Remember, building a life together is all about communication, compromise, and knowing what you can or cannot live with. When going over the six points below, don't assume the other person is simply going to change. Odds are, they're going to be pretty much the same person tomorrow that they are today.

VALUES

Everyone has religious, moral, spiritual, or other philosophical values that guide their lives. These values are important in making us the people we are. You need to decide if it's important for your spouse to have the same or similar values as yourself. Having the same religious beliefs and values was important to me, but for other people, it may not be a big deal. If you and your future spouse have very different values and philosophies about life, it's important that you support and tolerate each other's differences in this area.

When considering whether or not you could marry the man you're dating, ask yourself how you feel about things like drinking, smoking, white lies, drug use, pornography, and gambling. If your man had a problem with one of these, could you accept that problem, or would you have a hard time living with it?

Give your relationship a point if you have similar values and beliefs, or if you can support and tolerate the widower having different values and beliefs.

RECREATIONAL ACTIVITIES

What do you and the widower like to do in your spare time? Do you like to do the same things, or do you have different interests? Recreational activities aren't something you have to share, but you need to be able to support your spouse in whatever activities he or she chooses.

Julianna likes to run marathons. Training is very time-consuming. Even though I don't run marathons, I'm fully supportive of her. I'm more than happy to watch the kids for several hours on Saturday mornings so Julianna can do her long runs, or even put all the kids in the minivan and drive along the route to give her something to drink and encouragement every three miles along her training route. Similarly, Julianna knows I love writing. Even though she has no interest in writing, she understands that I need 60–90 minutes most days to write, and she goes out of her way to make sure I have it. (She's lying next to me in our bed, reading, as I write this chapter.)

Decide what sporting or recreational activities are important to you, and ask yourself if it's important that the widower participates in these activities with you. How would it affect you if participating in activities you enjoy or supporting you wasn't important to your spouse? What does "support" mean to you? Is he aware of that?

Give your relationship one point if you both enjoy the same recreational activities or, if they're different, you support each other in the things you choose to do.

Money

Money, or lack thereof, can be one of the big stressors in marriage. It's also one of the leading causes of divorce. When it comes to finances, you need to be in the same ballpark. There's always room for compromise, of course, but if one of you likes to spend money like there's no tomorrow, while the other person is more conservative, there's going to be a lot of stress in your marriage.

How do you feel about debt, paying bills, investments, savings, college funds, living month-to-month, and personal spending money? Does the widower feel the same way, or does he have a different view of finances? How much money must you have annually in order to feel that your needs have been met? Does the widower feel the same way? Are there any financial problems that you would or would not be willing to live with? Are you okay with separate checking accounts, or do you need to share one?

Julianna and I like to avoid debt and live within our means. The fact that we have the same views about money has saved us lots of stress. There have been times during our married life when money's been tight, and we've struggled to make ends meet. Because we're on the same page as far as spending, budgeting, and debt goes, we've been able to work together and get through the tight financial times with minimal marital stress. If financial stress is something you'd like to minimize, make sure that you and the widower are close to the same page, or can reach some happy middle ground.

Give your relationship one point if you have similar views of money and finances.

Sex

How important is it for you to be with someone who shares your sexual interests, beliefs, and desires?

Do you need to be with someone who can openly discuss sexual matters? Would you have a problem with the widower looking at pornography or masturbating? How often do you need to have sex? Would it cause a problem in your marriage if you weren't able to have sex as often as you desired? What sexual problems or performance issues would you be willing to live with?

If you're waiting until marriage to be intimate, does your future spouse share the same value? Can the two of you talk about sexual needs and wants before you're married? Are you willing to be patient with each other while you learn how best to please the other person?

Give your relationship one point if the widower meets your sexual needs, or has the same values when it comes to sex.

EDUCATION, INTELLIGENCE, AND WORK ETHIC

We all want to be with someone who is intellectually compatible with us and with whom we can have conversations. One thing to note is that *education* does not necessarily equal *intelligence*. Just because someone has a Ph.D. doesn't mean they have the ability to carry on an enjoyable conversation with you. Conversely, someone without a college education isn't necessarily an idiot. Nor does it mean that you have to have degrees in similar subjects. Julianna has a hard science degree, while I have a liberal arts degree. Despite these differences in interests, we're at similar intellectual levels, and are able to carry on conversations on a variety of subjects without any problems. If anything, our varied backgrounds and interests go a long way toward giving each other a different perspective on things. Whether you have similar or diverse intellectual interests, what's important is that you find someone on your intellectual level so you can talk to them about things. So ask yourself, what kind of intelligence and/or education do you need a spouse to have in order to respect him, and does your widower have what you need for an intellectually fulfilling relationship?

Additionally, what does he do for a living? How important is it for your spouse to be financially successful? If he or she lost their job, would you be okay living on less? Is it important to have your spouse home a lot, or would you mind if he or she worked late? How would business trips and long hours affect your relationship?

Give your relationship one point if the widower meets your educational, intellectual, and status needs.

FAMILY

We discussed blending families in Chapter 6, but I'm going to take it a bit further in this part of the book as it involves more than merging families and dealing with the late wife's parents. For example, some questions to ask yourself include the following: Do you need to be with someone who will put you first, before other family members or their dependent children? What roles do you need your spouse to assume to have a happy relationship? What step-parenting issues or problems are you willing to face? Is it important that your spouse likes family and is open to you spending a lot of time with them? Do you want more children? If so, how many? Does your spouse feel the same way?

This was the one area where Krista and I were different. We never matched up in the role we wanted our extended families to play in our lives, or in how many kids we wanted. As a result, 95 percent of the stress and arguments in my first marriage came from family-related issues. When I started dating again, I promised myself I wouldn't marry someone who didn't share my beliefs about family life. Thankfully, Julianna and I match perfectly. As a result, we have fewer fights and less stress in our marriage. Keep that compatibility in mind not only for this issue, but the other issues in this book too.

Give yourself one point if you and the widower have similar values and beliefs when it comes to families and parenting.

ADD THEM UP

If you feel that you and the widower are compatible in five out of six areas, odds are, the two of you have enough in common to make a marriage work. If you got less than five out of six, take a step back and decide if you're in a relationship that can last until you're both old and gray.

Remember, marrying a widower is like marrying anyone else, and there's more to the relationship than knowing he's ready to make room in his heart for you. It's about building a life together, and the more you can live together and work with each other, the better the chances of you growing old together. If you choose to move forward, do so without any doubts in your heart that it's the right thing to do.

You know your relationship better than anyone else. When thinking about growing old together, weigh and evaluate what you know. Trust your gut. Be honest with yourself, and your relationship can stand the test of time. I wish you the best of luck whatever you decide to do.

JULIANNA'S STORY

Out of all the men I dated, Abel was the only one who kept running with me. Every morning at 5:00 a.m., he'd knock on my door, and we'd head out for one of my training runs. Despite the fact that I never slowed down for him, Abel at least tried to keep up with me. Other men I dated gave up after a matter of weeks or days. But Abel was there every morning to support me.

His dedication helped me see a different side of Abel—one that didn't involve the loss of his wife and daughter. He knew that running was important to me, and he was willing to get up early to do what it took to support me in my goals. As I got to know him better, I realized that he had other qualities I wanted in a husband: he held similar values and beliefs, he was a hard worker, and he was someone I could talk to about anything and everything. The more time we spent together, the more I learned about him. Soon I realized that he was the man I wanted to spend the rest of my life—and eternity—with.

A part of me didn't want to marry a widower—no matter how wonderful he was. But the longer we've been married, the less important the widower-related issues have become. Instead, issues like faith, money, sex, family, and other things have become prominent. Thankfully, we both know we can trust each other on these issues and are heading in the same direction.

In the nine years we've been married, we've experienced the best of times and the worst of times. We've have periods of wealth, health, and plenty, and other times of unemployment, illness, and uncertainty. But because we're united on the important issues, we've been able to navigate the tough times side-by-side and